Evan Powell rocks it 20" style.

WARNING
Bike riding, even pump track riding, is potentially dangerous. Individual skills, tracks, conditions and equipment differ, and due to these unlimited factors beyond anyone's control, liabilty is expressly disclaimed. Do not attempt any techniques that are beyond your ability.

--- --- ---

Version 1.2 : July 23, 2008

First published as an ebook in 2006 by Lee Likes Bikes LLC, 2433 Linden Dr., Boulder CO 80304, USA.

For distribution and translation, contact Lee McCormack, lee@leelikesbikes.com.

ISBN 0974566012   EAN-13 9780974566016

--- --- ---

THANKS TO
My wife @b for supporting my madness, and letting me build The Best Pump Track Ever at the house we just bought. We have 1.5 acres to work with ... :)

ABOUT THE AUTHOR
Lee McCormack is a longtime journalist, rider, racer and instructor. He co-wrote the best-selling "Mastering Mountain Bike Skills," writes for numerous cycling magazines and runs www.leelikesbikes.com. He lives in Boulder, CO with his wife Arlette, two kids Kate and Ian, two dogs Rufus and Oscar, and cat Nola.

Check out **www.leelikesbikes.com**

Welcome to
Pump Track Nation

How to build and ride the best
pump track on Earth — Yours

By Lee McCormack

Race Line Publishing : Lee Likes Bikes LLC

Never have back yards been so much fun.

Contents

Fast Jon Watt takes to the suburban air.

Pump tracks are SO cool

Welcome to the wonderful world of Pump. Pump tracks are the hottest thing to sweep the world since probably the Hula Hoop. They're fun, and they make great training. Riders of all styles and levels can dig them, and even the neighbors get into it (if you have cool neighbors).

On my site I get lots of questions about designing and building pump tracks. I answer many questions on the site, but I thought it was time to put all of the essential info in one place. This ebook contains never-before-published information.

Special thanks to Steve Wentz, who started the North American pump track movement, and to my wife @b, who will soon let me ride in our new back yard.

What is a pump track

A pump track is a continuous loop that you can ride without pedaling. Yes, you actually gain speed — over 20 mph — by "pumping" rollers and berms. Most pump tracks are roughly oval, with cross-over lines. A few contain gap jumps, but the best use steep berms and smooth rollers to build speed and create smiles.

Know your pump track history

The first pump tracks were probably the dense BMX trails of the '70s and '80s. The modern pump track revolution traces to Australian downhillers. In 2003 a pro named Myles Mead told me about a track that slalomed downhill then looped back up — the guys were actually pumping rollers uphill. In 2005 Mick Hannah's steeply bermed backyard appeared in the movie Earthed 2, and the world saw its first pump track.

Steve Wentz was just ahead of the curve. In December 2004 the pro downhiller built a 150-foot-long L-shaped track at The Fix Bike Shop in Boulder, CO. At first nobody could even ride the ultratight corners, but soon the local crew was sweeping off the snow and ripping on a daily basis. I posted the track on my site, www.leelikesbikes.com, and the Pump Track Nation was born.

Emails poured in from all over the world: Thailand, Sweden, Malaysia, Australia and throughout the United States. Tracks popped up in parks, lots and yards. Ray's MTB in Cleveland, OH built an indoor two-lane pump track out of wood. This track was included in the 2006 3Ride Pro

"Pump tracks are the new horseshoes."
- Mark Weir, WTB pro racer and pump ambassador

"[Riding Lee's pump track] was a life changing experience."- Leanna Gerrard, Bear Naked/Cannondale pro racer

Invitational event – the first sanctioned pump track race. BTW, Brian Lopes killed it.

Lopes lookin' fat and slow in my back yard.

Why build one?

If you like bikes, and you have access to a small piece of land, you should build a pump track. That's all there is to it.

Pump tracks fit just about anywhere. They can be ridden by anyone. They are a ridiculously effective workout. They build skills like crazy. They improve other sports like skiing and motocross. They bring cool people together. They stop the erosion of the modern family. And they are really, really fun.

Convincing the authorities

Not everyone thinks the way we do. Poor souls. If you find yourself struggling to close the deal with your parents/government/spouse, try slinging these stones:

- Less maintenance, water and chemistry than a lawn. Xeriscape with a purpose.

- Great technique training. For bikes, skis, snowboard, moto or anything like that.

- Great for overall fitness.

- Great for mental strength. Focus, discipline, confidence. Your grades will improve.

- Keeps you near home, near your beloved family. Family values!

- Hours and hours of fun in a safe, healthy environment.

- It can still look really nice. Flagstones in the infield, flowers on the berms … Better Homes and Pump Tracks, baby!

Choosing a location

You don't need a lot of space. You can make a sweet track with as little as 20x30 feet of ground. You can rock hard with 50x50. Odd shapes work fine. Go crazy!

The ideal site is very slightly sloped so rain drains away. If you live in a housing development, your back yard is probably just right. Bone flat is OK. A steeper slope can be worked with.

Make sure you have permission! If it's your back yard, sweet. If it's someone else's property, promise something cool in return — like all the hot chicks who will hang out watching the pump masters. Yeah, baby!

Read your HOA covenants. Few will say exactly, "no pump tracks," but your neighbors can make trouble. My old neighbors hated the fact I was having fun in the neighborhood, and so they complained to our homeowners association. I received a letter:

> *"Dear Mr. McCormack,*
>
> *We've received numerous complaints about the condition of your back yard. You cannont rip up your lawn and build a bike track. That violates our covenants. ..."*

Of course, the covenants failed to say "no pump tracks." I carefully read the covenants and crafted my response:

Petr Hanak in Winter Park, CO. He got permission from this landowner.

> *Let me assure you that I too am committed to maintaining the appearance and value of properties in this neighborhood.*
>
> *To re-quote Section 10 of the covenants:*
>
> *"... After a residence has been constructed on any lot, the remaining unpaved portion of the lot shall promptly be planted to [sic] grass or other vegetation or covered with decorative materials, and maintained in that condition, so as to prevent the blowing of dust and dirt from the exposed soil."*
>
> *I am in the process of xeriscaping my back yard to create a useful, attractive space that uses minimal water and chemicals. At this time the cold weather and frozen ground prohibit further landscaping work. When the weather warms and the ground softens, I will finish the project in accordance with the covenants.*
>
> *Until that time, I will make sure any exposed dirt is sufficiently packed and/or moistened to prevent blowing dust.*
>
> *I appreciate everyone's concern for our fine neighborhood. If you*

need anything, please don't hesitate to ask.

Sincerely,

Lee McCormack

Ha! Take that.

I covered the infields with flagstone, and everything was cool.

Two key ideas

Smoothness. Think of a sine wave. Your pump track should have continuous curves, with smooth ups, downs, lefts and rights. There should be no flat ground, no abrupt edges. The whole track is a sculpture: a study in constancy and flow.

Do it right the first time: This cannot be overemphasized. The more work you put into each roller and berm, the better it'll ride and the longer it'll last. Don't rush the project. Build each component perfectly before you move on. Pile. Pack. Water. Repeat.

Grading and drainage

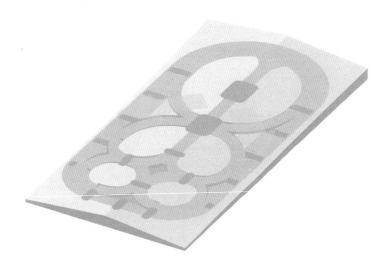

You need to move water off the track without creating so steep a slope the track becomes hard to ride. An overall grade of 2-3 percent is ideal. This diagram is based on a 2 percent grade.

In housing, the standard grade is 2% away from the house. A usable area can be up to about 5%. (Source: David Ignatew, landscape architect)

Here's an example:

The top of the track is the highest point.

The middle of the track (going lengthwise) is slightly higher than the sides.

Water sheets from the top to the bottom and from the mid line to the outside.

To keep water from pooling in the inside berms, drains carry water below the track to the outside. Very shallow culverts (just a few inches deep, with soft edges) will water along the surface without creating a hazard.

Do it French style

If you have a flat yard, and especially if you use your own dirt, water will want to collect in the low spots. Dig deep ditches on the insides of berms and on the sides of the troughs. Fill the ditches with gravel. Set a grate on top, and seal the gravel with Quickcrete. Make sure the infield and the track drain toward your French drains. Sweet!

Watering

Your pump track will need water. You'll use a lot of water in the building phase, and the track will need regular watering to set up a hard surface and to keep dust down. I suggest:

A hose – Essential while you're building, and acceptable for maintenance.

Sprinklers – Excellent for maintenance. You can set a timer so the track gets 15 minutes of water at 5 a.m. Sweet!

Pump tracks need water the way plants do. In the beginning, water your track every time you ride. Get it wet, let it dry most of the way, then ride! Over time the riding surface will pack as hard as rock.

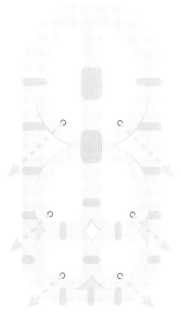

The inside berms need pipes or French drains.

You'll need these tools

Earth-moving equipment – To place the dirt in rough piles. Or see below.

Round-bladed shovel – Spend at least $50 on a good one. You and this shovel will become best friends. Or worst enemies.

Tamper, sod roller, ATV, feet, etc. – To compact the dirt.

Tape measure – If you're the kind of person who washes his hands a lot. Measure twice, dig once!

Giant compass – A stake and rope to mark turns, if you're as compulsive as I am!

Water – The key to a durable, fast track.

Patience – This is a major project! No matter what, building a track is a very physical endeavor. By the time you build the track, you'll be strong enough to ride it.

Wrap your shovel handle with sports tape, like a hockey stick.

Jon Watt rips endemic dirt.

Sweet trails are often called "loamy." Now you know what that means.

Let's talk dirt

OK, are you going to use your own dirt (let's call it endemic so we seem smart), or are you gonna import dirt? Each has its advantages:

Endemic dirt

- Cheap

- Easy to reverse

Imported dirt

- Maintain current grade

- Choose great soil

- Less work than digging up your yard

If you use your own dirt

Take out every rock, root and shell casing. Remove sod, or at least break it up until it mixes into the dirt. Any chunk will cause a cave-in later on. You want perfect homogeneity, just like in American society.

If you buy dirt

Bring in some good topsoil. It's easy to work with, sets up a great riding surface and drains well. Topsoil or "loam" is a combination of sand, silt, clay and organic matter. Most loam has a pretty even mix of these materials. Clay loam has a higher proportion of clay, and it tends to pack best (and make the best tracks). SO: When you order dirt, ask for clay loam or topsoil with some clay mixed in.

How much dirt will you need?

You'll order soil by the cubic yard. To estimate the amount, try this:

Length x Width x Average height / 27 = Cubic yards

Multiply cubic yards by 1.3 to account for soil compaction.

To get the average height, figure half the height of your rollers and berms. For example:

150ft x 4ft x 1ft / 27 = 22 cubic yards

22 x 1.3 = 29 cubic yards

Get more than you think you'll need. You'll find a use for it.

Laying out your track

Post this on your refrigerator: Measure twice, dig once.

I cannot overstress the importance of planning your track. If you just start digging you WILL dig yourself into a corner, and you'll end up making compromises — or starting over. No fun!

You can be as creative as you like. But you'll save serious hassle if you follow these guidelines:

No flat spots: Every square inch should tilt up, down or sideways. You can't pump flat ground; keep it moving!

Make the berms tall and steep: You can generate close to three Gs, and to rail that hard you need a 70-degree bank.

Make the rollers low and smooth: Many builders go too tall and steep, which is very difficult to pump quickly. Keep your rollers down to about 16 inches tall, with gradual faces.

Smooooth ...

Make it versatile: Sets of rollers can be pumped, manualed or jumped in myriad combinations. Gap jumps are cool I guess, but that's a different deal.

Consider drainage: So many sweet tracks become swimming pools in winter. If you have a slope, use shallow ditches and pipes to route water off the track. If you're working on flat ground, dig holes in your low spots and fill them with gravel. French drain style.

Start simple: Build an outside loop first. Get that dialed, then add cross-overs to multiply the options.

If you start a feature, finish it. Devote enough time each day to complete one berm, set of rollers, etc. If you leave a feature undone, the dirt gets dry and crappy.

Do it right the first time: This cannot be overemphasized. The more work you put into each roller and berm, the better it'll ride and the longer it'll last. Don't rush the project. Build each component perfectly before you move on. Pile. Pack. Water. Repeat.

Get ready to work: The pump track in my yard took 50 man-hours of hard labor. It was definitely worth it.

Don't begin the Greatest Pump Track on Earth only to lose focus and end up with crap. This happens all the time.

Lopes rails. Radius = 11 feet.

Building berms

Good berms are easy to ride, and they let you generate mega speed.

Radius. The tighter the turn, the harder it is to make, but the more pump it gives you. Six- to 10-foot turns are the funnest overall, but a few 3-footers keep things interesting.

Tight: 3 feet - Experts only!

Medium: 6 feet - Good all around.

Wide: 10-12 feet - Fast!

Banking. When you rip a turn, your speed and the radius of the turn combine in a mathematical blender to create the cornering Gs and your lean angle. For example, if you ride 15 mph through a 15-foot-radius turn, you generate 1G and lean 45 degrees (the turning force and gravity average each other out; see diagram).

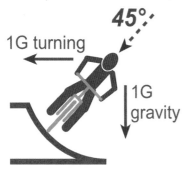

Our goal is to always press the tires directly into the ground. This way, we don't need traction between the tire and the dirt — it's like we're riding a roller coaster (as a matter of fact, roller coaster designers use the same equations).

Your berms should have smooth banks that transition gradually from flat to about 55-60 degees (the steeper, the better — dirt is usually the limiting factor). The main worn line will be at 30-35 degrees; this corresponds to a turn of 0.6Gs (a nice sports car). A 60° top bank will let riders pull up to 2Gs without sliding; beyond that the bike will drift — but if you're pulling 3G turns like a pro, you can handle it!

1. Mark your arc. Make a giant compass out of a stake and some string. Measure your radius, plant the stake and mark your arc with paint, chalk, etc. Your main riding line will end up on or near this mark.

2. Pile dirt around your arc. Start piling it about 2 feet outside your mark.

If you dig up your yard, stand on the inside of the turn and pile dirt to the outside.

3. Keep piling until the dirt is at least 50% taller than the envisioned berm (you'll be compacting the dirt). Your outside berms will be three feet tall, so shoot for a pile 4.5 feet tall. Yeah, that's a lot of dirt!

4. Working from the top down, slide the loose dirt down the face to get the shape you want.

It's almost impossible to get a nice shape by *adding* dirt; it's much easier to *move* dirt. Let gravity help you.

5. Pack as you go. Give it a little flat top. The riding surface should be rock hard and super smooth. When you get the shape you want, water it and let it sit overnight.

A berm is a lot like a roller, only it's really wide (and curved). Make your berm as tall and steep as possible in the middle, then let it taper toward the ends. There you will build rollers.

Wolverine with a little double-manual action.

If you dig up your yard, build rollers from hole-dirt.

Building rollers

These lumps of dirt are so sweet and versatile. You can roll over 'em, pump 'em, manual 'em or even jump 'em. All rollers are fun to ride, but the best are:

Consistent. Make sets of equally tall, evenly spaced rollers. This lets you find a rhythm.

Not too tall or close. The most common mistake is building rollers too tall, too steep and too close together. This feels OK at low speeds, but when you get going fast they'll really ball you up.

1:10 ratio. If your rollers are one foot tall, they shoul dbe 10 feet apart. This height:length ratio is relatively easy to ride, yet it provides excellent pump and speed. You can make your rollers taller and closer. Just know your track will be trickier to ride.

Width: Single lanes 2-3 feet. Interchanges 4-6 feet.

1. Build your berms first. Place the first rollers right at the ends of the berms, where the curves turn to the straight. Space the other roller(s) evenly along the straight.

2. Pile dirt on the marks. Keep piling until the dirt is about 50% higher than the desired rollers. If you want your roller to be six feet wide on the riding surface (top), make your pile about eight feet wide.

3. Working from the top, slide the dirt down to make smooth transitions. Remember: We're talking about a sine wave here

4. As you get the shape you want, pack the dirt like crazy. Extend the top of the berm so it goes all the way to the roller.

Smooth and pack the sides of the rollers as well. Water your gems thoroughly and let them sit overnight.

When your roller abuts a berm, shape the slopes to they smoothly transition into each other. Viewed from the side, the roller would still be a perfect roller; there just happens to be a berm on one side of it.

2.

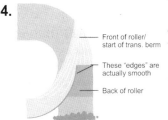

3.

4.

Front of roller/
start of trans. berm

These "edges" are
actually smooth

Back of roller

Building interchanges

Crossover lines add options and fun galore, and they let you turn in more than one direction. This ain't Nascar!

Interchanges from outside berms to crossovers

1. Finish the berms on the ends of the straights.

2. Mark the inside berm. Mark the rollers for the entire straight. Your interchange berms will be next to rollers. You will build these berms and rollers together.

3. Begin to pile and shape the interchange berm and roller.

The interchange berm and roller should flow smoothly from the outside berm. The front of the roller is part of the outside berm, which is part of the transition berm, which is the front of the roller … It's a complex 3D shape!

4. Do the final shaping, packing and watering. Finish the other roller on the straight. Water, wait a day then ride!

5. Finish the other rollers on the straight.

OUTSIDE BERM

ROLLER

TRANS. BERM

(This track has a 2-way trans. berm)

Interchanges from side straights to crossovers

1. Finish the outside berms on the ends of the straights, as well as interchanges from the outside berms.

2. Mark the inside berm. Your rollers should already be marked. Your interchange berms will be near rollers. You will build these berms and rollers together.

3. Begin to pile and shape the interchange berm and roller. The berm will "point" into the straight, like a freeway off-ramp.

4. Do the final shaping, packing and watering.

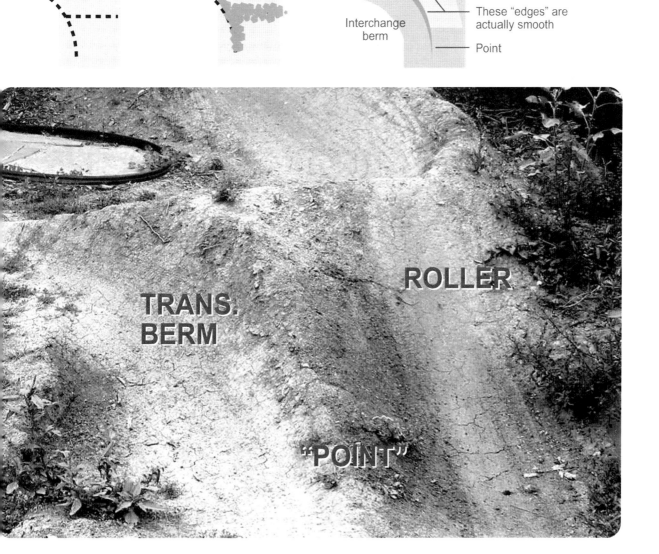

Build in this order

1. Grading, drainage and sprinklers

2. Outside berms

3. Outside straights, including rollers and interchanges

4. Inside berms

5. Inside straights, rollers and interchanges

6. Bandstands, concessions, media center

Good shovel technique …

… saves time and energy.

1. Holding the shovel high on its handle, place the point where you like.

2. Jump high onto the shovel, driving it deep into the ground.

3. Standing on the shovel, wiggle the handle until the blade is fully embedded.

4. Lean back to dislodge a big, juicy clump of earth.

5. Grip closer to the blade and place your treasure where you like.

Repeat a zillion times. You can easily maintain a good aerobic heart rate – I know 'cause I've worn my monitor!

Petr *PINS IT* on his track.

Riding your track

Pumping is simple: Just absorb any surface that faces the way you're coming from, and push into any surface that faces the way you want to go. Part of this push gets translated into forward motion and, voila, you gain speed. You can pump any bump: rocks, logs, water bars or curbs. A pump track is a laboratory for non-pedal propulsion: A loop of rollers and berms that can be ripped around without turning the cranks.

You start by working the rollers. Light, heavy, pull, push. You hit a corner hard and gain speed. The next set of rollers approaches fast. Too fast to roll – better manual. Pump another berm and you've reached 20 mph. Too fast to manual – better jump. You might hit a dozen rollers and four berms in less than 10 seconds. The workout is total, the speed is real and the possibilities are endless. Here are some basic tips to get you started.

It's all about position

Everything fun on a bike starts with the neutral attack position:

Centered fore-aft. Weight balanced completely on your feet. Hands weightless.

Centered up-down. Hips halfway between standing and hitting your seat.

Back flat. Torso level.

Head up. Look at the next turn. Yes, all the way out there.

Elbows out. It's solid, and it helps you whip your bike around.

This is the A-1 key to all riding. Practice until it becomes automatic.

High in the trough, low on the roller. Check out the low attack position.

Pump rollers

You're a bouncing sine wave. The rollers are one sine wave, and you're another. As you ride, bounce up and down (with your feet) so you're light on the front of the bump and very heavy on back of the bump. You basically take the wave of your energy and shift it just a bit ahead of the bump wave.

Don't touch the fronts. Loft your front wheel over every frontside, and push HARD down every backside. This is a lot of work, but it builds so much speed you'll freak out the first time you succeed.

Rigid bike

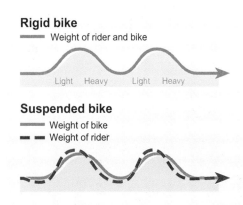

Suspended bike

You are a floating head. Try to keep your head and torso flowing in a level line. Use your arms and legs to pull and push as you go. You are a killer death lizard from Pump Island.

The lower the better. At the top of each roller, the lower you are on your bike (or the higher the bike is – trip out on that) the more range of motion you have for the pump.

Use them legs. Compress on the tops. Extend in the troughs. Let your arms go along for the ride.

Remember your attack position!

Rip berms

Look through the *exit* of the turn. Yes — this is so key!

Lean your bike. It's the only way to make a turn.

Wolverine with the perfect head turn. He's looking at the roller exiting this berm.

Trust the berm. As long as your tires are pressing directly into the ground,

You can do (almost) no wrong.

A berm is a hole turned on its side. Enter low. Extend and press into the first part. Absorb the "front side" on the way out.

Ready for the roller. There should be a roller right at the exit. You've unweighted to leave the berm — use that lightness to get over the roller! Then pump the heck out of it.

Remember your attack position!

It's a fresh start

Pump tracking totally applies to "real" mountain biking, but it's so unique it's almost a completely different sport. And this can be a good thing.

As we ride over the years, many of us develop bad habits. We learn these habits because they seem to serve us. We stiffen up when we reach bumps, so we can protect ourselves. We keep our bikes upright in corners, so we don't fall over. These habits actually detract from our riding, but every time you hit a bump stiff and survive, or take a turn upright and stay on two wheels, that counts as a success. Not as a riding success, but as a survival success.

So our brains say "Sweet, that totally worked!" and the habits become more and more ingrained.

The only way to erase those etchings is to practice – no, exaggerate – proper technique. Staying loose in bumps, leaning your bike in turns: that sort of stuff.

A pump track is a laboratory. It's non-threatening, and it's so different from normal riding that it allows you to ride your bike with an entirely new mindset.

Pro XC dominatrix Judy Freeman gets her pump on.

Joey's all perfect,except for that tuft of hair.

If you've suffered too much stress over the years on your XC bike, ride your pump track on a different bike. Use flat pedals. Wear a t-shirt and baggy shorts. Leave your heart rate monitor in your shrine.

Play.

Exaggerate. Pick a key technique and beat it to death. Ride with open fingers. Try to look two turns ahead. Completely straighten your inside arm.

Experiment. Try different positions and lines. Push here, pull there. If it works you'll accelerate immediately. If not, well, try something else.

Be cool. If you fall into any old self-hating behaviors, STOP! Chill out. Come back with a sense of play.

Pump tracking is fun for its own sake, but if you take advantage of this opportunity it'll improve all of your riding.

Enjoy the process

As you get faster through the rollers, you'll progress from pumping them to manualing them and finally to jumping them. Super fun.

Lory State Park in Fort Collins, CO, has a sweet pump track.

Pump tracks: I can't think of a better way to improve your riding and have a great time.

The Fix/Rhythmn Cycles pump track

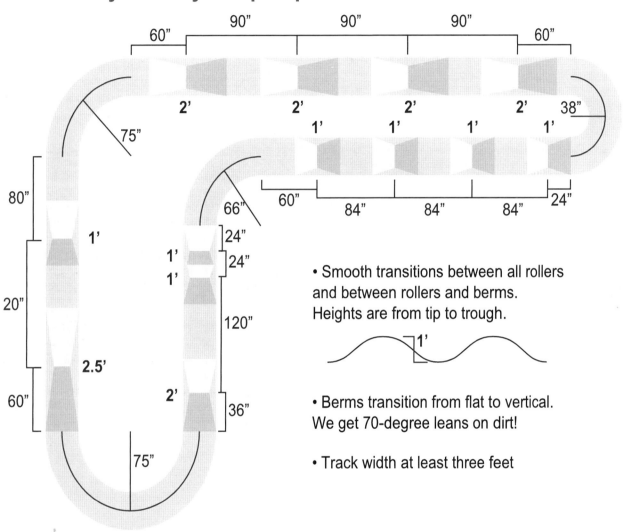

- Smooth transitions between all rollers and between rollers and berms. Heights are from tip to trough.

- Berms transition from flat to vertical. We get 70-degree leans on dirt!

- Track width at least three feet

Lee's (ex) pump track

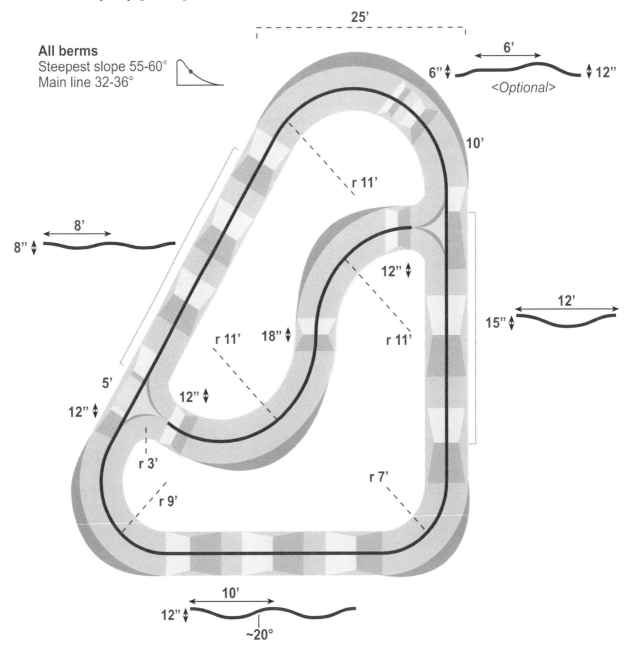

All berms
Steepest slope 55-60°
Main line 32-36°

25'

6'
6" ↕ ↕ 12"
<Optional>

10'

r 11'

8'
8" ↕

12" ↕

18" ↕

r 11'

r 11'

12" ↕

5'

12'
15" ↕

12" ↕

r 3'

r 9'

r 7'

10'
12" ↕
~20°

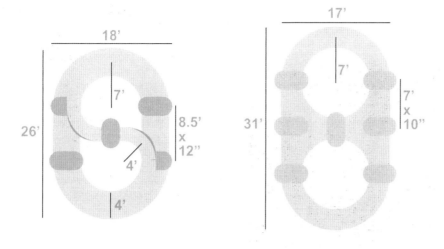

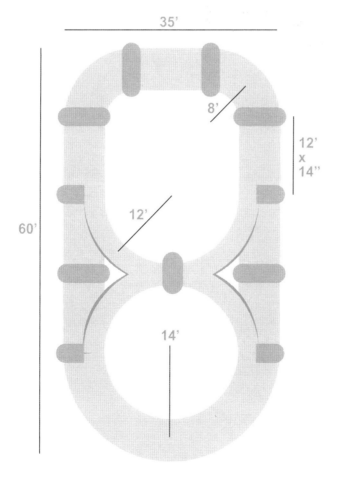

Pumping uphill

Yes, you can build a pump track on a slope. The pump track in Winter Park, CO goes straight up a 10% slope — and, believe it or not, you can go really fast! Here are some ideas.

See more tracks at http://www.leelikesbikes.com/category/cool-rides/pump-tracks/

BICYCLE TRACK LIABILITY WAIVER AND RELEASE OF LIABILITY

WARNING: BICYCLING IS A DANGEROUS ACTIVITY. BY ENGAGING IN THIS ACTIVITY, THE PARTICIPANT ASSUMES THE RISK OF SERIOUS INJURY OR DEATH. THIS IS A RELEASEOF LIABILITY—YOU MUST READ AND FULLY UNDERSTAND THIS BEFORE SIGNING. IF YOU ARE UNDER 18, YOUR PARENT OR LEGAL GUARDIAN MUST SIGN THIS WAIVER.

Participant Name: _____

Address:

_____

_____

I, THE NAMED PARTICIPANT, for myself and on behalf of my/our heirs, assigns, personal representatives and next of kin, hereby acknowledge that I voluntarily have applied to participate and use the Bicycle Track. I understand that the act of bicycling necessaril involves known and unknown risks of injury to me and other people, which includes but is not limited to death, permanent or temporary paralysis, disability, illness or disease, physical or mental damage, or other injury, as well as damage to my equipment and personal property. Some of these risks include the risks inherent in bicycling such as falling and coming into contact with berms, rollers and other object, latent or apparent defects or conditions in equipment or property, and passive or active negligent acts of myself, _____ (Below referred to as TRACK OWNER), other riders, Race Line Publishing and Lee Likes Bikes LLC. I understand that the above list of risks is not complete or exhaustive and that those and other risks known or unknown, anticipated or unanticipated may also result in injury, death, illness, disease to myself or my property or other third parties. I voluntarily agree and promise to accept and assume responsibilities, and injuries, death, illness, disease or damage to myself or my property arising from my participation in this activity.

I further understand that TRACK OWNER assumes no liability for loss, damage, or any kind of injury sustained by myself or my property while using the Bicycle Track. I therefore assume all risks associated with using the Bicycle Track, even if they arise from the negligence of TRACK OWNER, other riders, Race Line Publishing and Lee Likes Bikes LLC. My participation in this activity is voluntary and no one is forcing me to participate in spite of the risks. I understand the effect of this waiver and acceptance of risk on my legal rights.

By signing this release of liability and using the Bicycle Track, I hereby fully and forever release and discharge indemnify and hold harmless TRACK OWNER and all associates from any and all liabilities, claims, demands, damages, rights of action, suits or causes of action present of future, whether they same be known or unknown, anticipated or unanticipated, resulting from or arising out of my use or intended use of said Bicycle Track premises, facilities or equipment. I fully and forever release and discharge TRACK OWNER and associates from any and all negligent acts and omissions in the same, and intend to be legally bound by this release.

Name of participant using facility: _____

Date of birth: _____/_____/_____

Signature of participant using facility: _____

Today's Date ____/____/_____

Phone (_____)_____-_____

Driver's License #_____

FOR PARTICIPANTS UNDER 18 YEARS OF AGE

This is to certify that I, as a parent or guardian with legal responsibility for the above named participant, to consent and ratify his/her release of the TRACK OWNER, and other riders, I release and agree to indemnify the TRACK OWNER, and all associates from any and all liabilities incident to my minor child's involvement or participation in the Skate Park as provided above, even if arising from the negligence of the TRACK OWNER, and its associates, to the fullest extent permitted by law. I have carefully read this release of liability and understand and fully agree with its contents.

If the participant is under 18, this release must be signed in person by a parent/legal guardian, or their signature must be acknowledged by a notary public.

I hereby certify that I am the parent or legal guardian of the participant named above, give my consent to the foregoing, and agree to hold the Bicycle Track harmless from any liability

_____

Parent or Legal Guardian

Parent/Guardian's Driver's License #_____

Subscribed and sworn to before me this _____day of _____, 200 ___

_____Notary Public (Seal)

My commission expires on _____.

A smooth track feels superfast on a BMX bike.
Lee rocks his Intense cruiser in Denver, CO.

Made in the USA
Lexington, KY
12 May 2012